DUGONGS

Geoff Miller

Grolier
an imprint of

www.scholastic.com/librarypublishing

Published 2009 by Grolier
An Imprint of Scholastic Library Publishing
Old Sherman Turnpike
Danbury, Connecticut 06816

For The Brown Reference Group
Project Editor: Jolyon Goddard
Picture Researchers: Clare Newman, Sophie
Mortimer
Designer: Sarah Williams
Managing Editor: Tim Harris

Volume ISBN-13: 978-0-7172-8066-7
Volume ISBN-10: 0-7172-8066-7

**Library of Congress
Cataloging-in-Publication Data**

Nature's children. Set 6.
    p. cm.
  Includes index.
  ISBN-13: 978-0-7172-8085-8
  ISBN-10: 0-7172-8085-3
  1. Animals--Encyclopedias, Juvenile. 1.
Grolier (Firm)
  QL49.N387 2009
  590.3--dc22
                      2008014675

Printed and bound in China

PICTURE CREDITS

Front Cover: **Oxford Scientific Films**:
David B. Fleetham.

Back Cover: **Oxford Scientific Films**: David
B. Fleetham, Mark Webster; **Photolibrary**:
Tobias Bernhard, Perrine Doug.

Ardea: Ben Cropp 32–33, 34, Nick Gordon
46, Parer and E. Parer-Cook 9, 14, 25;
Corbis: Tobias Bernhard 2–3, Natalie Fobes
13, Roger Garwood and Trish Ainslie 18,
Lawson Wood 42; **Oxford Scientific
Films**: David B. Fleetham 6, 17, 29, Andrea
Ghisotti 37, 38; **NHPA**: A.N.T. Photo Library
21, 22, 26, 41, B. Jones and M. Shimlock 45,
Trevor McDonald 10; **Still Pictures**: Kelvin
Aitken 5, D. Burton 4.

Contents

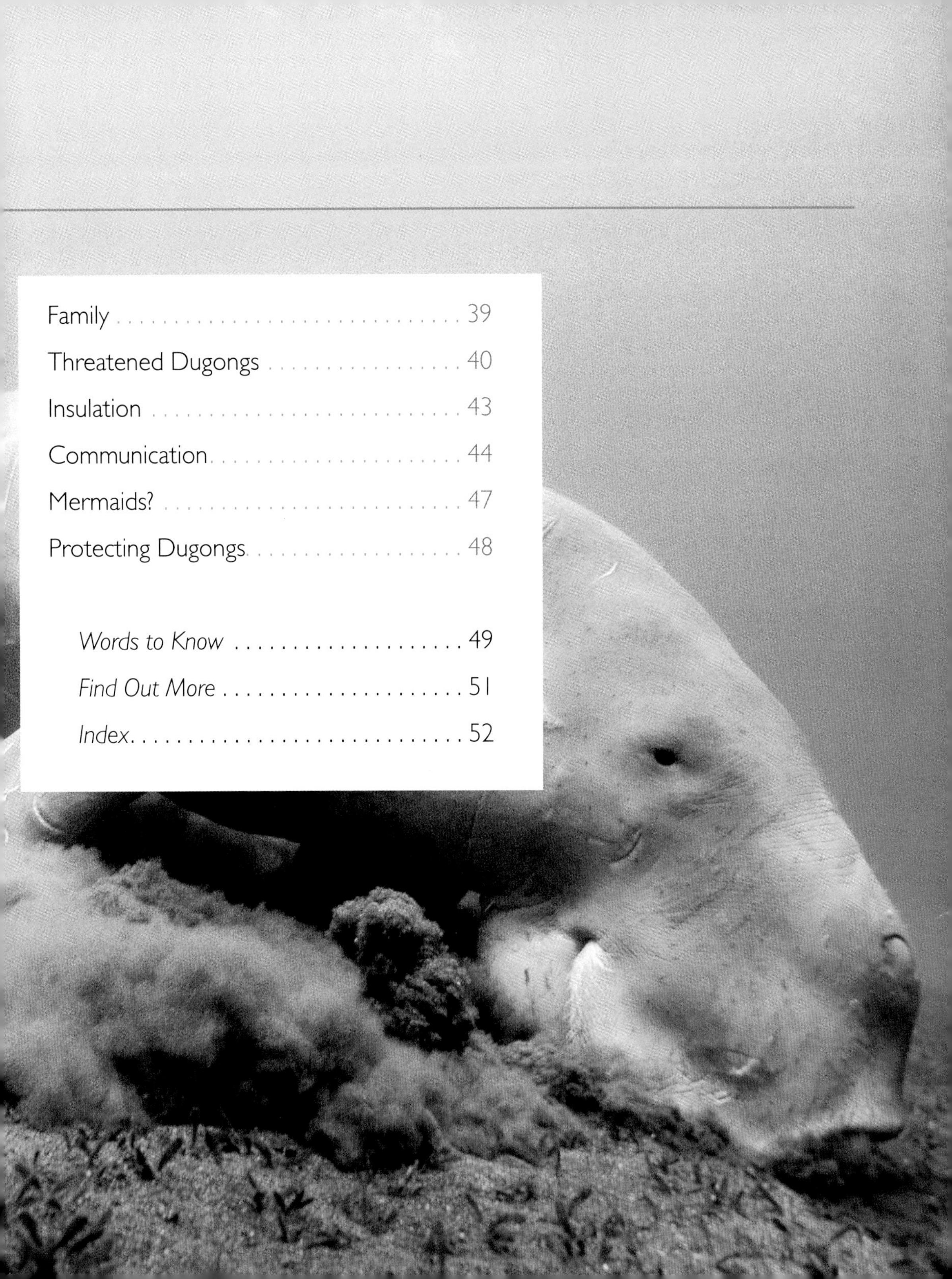

FACT FILE: Dugongs

Class	Mammals (Mammalia)
Order	Dugongs and manatees (Sirenia)
Family	Dugongidae
Genus	*Dugong*
Species	Dugongs (*Dugong dugon*)
World distribution	The coastal areas of the Pacific and Indian oceans, in the tropics and subtropics
Habitat	Warm, shallow coastal waters
Distinctive physical characteristics	Streamlined body; large, horizontal tail flukes and rounded front flippers; prominent downward-facing snout for bottom-feeding; small eyes; no visible ears
Habits	Dugongs live alone or in small family groups of males, females, and juveniles; they form strong bonds with their young
Diet	Sea grasses and other aquatic vegetation

Introduction

Dugongs are **mammals** that spend their whole
life in water. Unlike other sea mammals, such
as seals, whales, and dolphins, dugongs do not
eat other animals. Instead, these gentle animals
eat sea grasses and other plants that grow in the
shallow waters near the coast. Dugongs live in
the warm waters of the southwestern Pacific
Ocean. The dugong's closest relatives are
the manatees. Manatees look very much like
dugongs and have a similar lifestyle. However,
they live in a different part of the world.
Dugongs' and manatees' closest land relatives
are, in fact, elephants!

**A dugong searches for
sea grass on the seabed.**

Dugongs are the gentle giants of the world's tropical oceans.

Gentle Giants

Dugongs are one of the most rare—and least known—of all sea creatures. Most people are familiar with whales, dolphins, and sharks from aquariums, films, and books. However, dugongs are less often written about or held in captivity.

Dugongs are large, timid animals that swim in tropical waters. They look somewhat like seals. However, dugongs are much larger, with a plump, rounded body, small eyes, **flippers**, and a large tail like a whale's. These gentle giants eat only plants, so they are not a threat to other animals.

Range

Dugongs live in the tropical and subtropical areas of the Indian and Pacific oceans, close to the **equator**. These waters are warm all year round. Dugongs can be found from Africa's eastern coast eastward to the Red Sea and Sri Lanka, an island off the southern coast of India. Dugongs also live around the islands of Indonesia and parts of the South Pacific. Some of the largest populations of dugongs are found in the waters around Australia.

Dugongs don't venture far out to sea. Instead, they stay in the shallow waters near the coastline. Sadly, in some of these places dugongs have been hunted almost to the point of **extinction**.

A dugong herd swims in the waters of Shark Bay, off the coast of Western Australia.

9

This mother Caribbean
manatee and her calf live
off the coast of Florida.

Manatees

Dugongs are very closely related to another type of **marine** mammal called a manatee. One type, or **species**, of manatee lives off the southern coast of the United States—the Caribbean manatee. Together, dugongs and manatees belong in a group, or order, of animals known as Sirenia (SI-REH-NEE-UH). Sirenians are big, bulky-looking animals that grow to 10 feet (3 m) long or more and weigh more than 440 pounds (200 kg)—as much as three adult humans put together. Their large body is mostly made up of thick layers of fat, which help keep the animals warm. Dugongs live only in the sea. However, some species of manatees live in both saltwater and freshwater.

Steller's Sea Cow

Today, there are four species of sirenians. Long ago, there was a fifth, called Steller's sea cow. The sea cow was the biggest of all the sirenians. It was about 23 feet (7 m) long and weighed several tons. These sea cows lived in the cold, icy waters of the Arctic, where the continents of North America and Asia almost meet. Back then, sailors captured these mammals for their meat. Later, hunters killed sea cows in great numbers for their meat and fat. In a short time, Steller's sea cows had been hunted to extinction.

People occasionally mistake narwhals and whales, such as this gray whale surfacing in the Arctic Ocean, for dugongs.

Dugongs, like other marine mammals, must regularly come up to the surface to breathe.

Sea Mammals

Although they live in the sea, dugongs are not fish. They are mammals. Mammals are animals that breathe air, give birth to live young, and produce milk to feed their **offspring**. Most mammals live on the land. But dugongs are marine, or **aquatic**, mammals—like whales and dolphins—and spend all their life at sea. Fish breathe through **gills** that take oxygen from the water. But dugongs must regularly fill their lungs with air.

One way to easily tell a fish from a marine mammal is by looking at its tail. Fish's tails are vertical, or up and down, while dugongs' and other sea mammals' tails are horizontal, or level with the water's surface.

Over Time

Millions of years ago, dugongs and other marine mammals lived on dry land. Over a very long time, they moved from the land to live in the sea. This process is called **evolution**. Very, very slowly the marine mammal's body changed to suit its new conditions. It became more **streamlined**, and what once were front legs became flippers. Rear limbs eventually disappeared completely. They were replaced by large tail **flukes** more suitable for life in the water. Gradually, these creatures **adapted** to their new environment and became completely at home in the water.

Scientists think that dugongs
and manatees evolved from
a common ancestor that lived
in the western Atlantic Ocean
more than 35 million years ago.

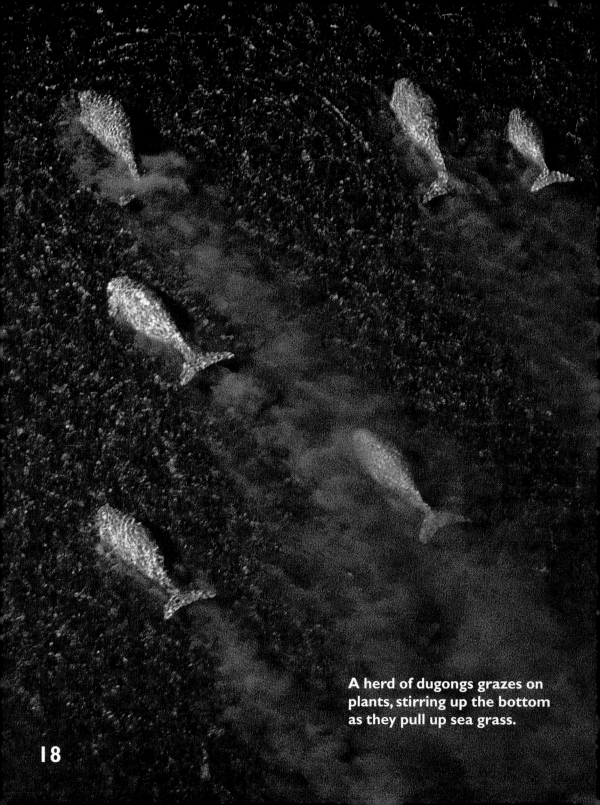

A herd of dugongs grazes on plants, stirring up the bottom as they pull up sea grass.

Sea Cows

Dugongs are **herbivores**, which means they eat only plants. They never prey on, or hunt, other animals for food. Instead they **graze** grasses and other aquatic plants that grow on the sea floor. In some parts of the world, a dugong is called a "sea cow." That is probably because of the animal's habit of grazing the seabed. Dugongs are well adapted to seabed feeding. Their muzzle, or snout, faces downward. This helps them stay in a horizontal swimming position as they patrol the ocean floor. Sometimes, dugongs tear up whole plants by their roots, digging them out with their flippers and snout. An adult dugong can eat as much as 30 pounds (14 kg) or more of plants every day.

Grazing

The ocean floor is covered in sand and mud.
When a dugong digs up one of its favorite
plants, it might need to clean it before eating
it. Using its snout and flippers, the dugong
removes most of the mud and sand, sometimes
shaking the plant vigorously to get the dirt off.
Sand and mud would irritate the dugong's
sensitive mouth. The grit would cause the
dugong's teeth to wear down.

Dugongs "prepare" their food another way,
too. They dig up the plant and roots and put
them in a pile and leave it. Later, when all the
sand and dirt has washed off, the dugong
returns to eat it. Sea grasses and other plants
are difficult to **digest**, so a dugong's stomach
is specially equipped for the job. It contains
thousands of tiny microorganisms, called
bacteria, which help break down the plant fibers.

A dugong uses its snout to dig up plants from the seabed.

A dugong dives to the ocean floor, where it will use its molar teeth to crush and grind tough sea plants.

Teeth and Tusks

Dugongs have teeth called **molars** that are ideal for crushing and grinding food. Molars help dugongs chew the rough-textured leaves and stems they eat. They start life with 24 teeth, but as dugongs grow older, some of their teeth fall out. Dugongs can still chew their food even after they have lost most of their teeth. Special tough, bony plates that protect the gums act as substitute teeth. When male dugongs reach 10 to 12 years old, two very different teeth start to grow down from the upper jaw. These extra-large pointed teeth look like tusks. This is one trait that dugongs and manatees share with their distant cousins, elephants.

Breathing

Dugongs can hold their breath underwater for about 8 to 10 minutes, perhaps even longer. Every now and then, though, they have to interrupt their grazing of the seabed and return to the water's surface for air. Although they can stay down longer, dugongs usually come up for air every couple of minutes. Once they are at the water's surface, a few seconds is all that's required for a quick breath before returning to the seabed. Sometimes, they make a distinct sound as they release the stale air from their lungs. They then take in a fresh breath and prepare for another dive.

Dugongs come to
the surface to breathe
every few minutes.

A dugong spurts spray from its nostrils as it surfaces.

Specialized Nose

A dugong breathes air in and out through two little holes at the top of its snout. These tiny openings are the dugong's nostrils. After a long dive, the nostrils are the first part of the dugong's body to emerge from the water. That way, as soon as the dugong reaches the water's surface it is able to take a breath. The nostrils' position on the snout also allows the dugongs to swim along and breathe at the same time, with only the top of the head poking above the water. A dugong can even rest and sleep like that. When it dives beneath the water, special valves close tightly over the dugong's nostrils to prevent water from getting in.

Slow and Steady

A dugong's sleek, smooth body helps it glide effortlessly through the water. It propels itself forward using its tail, which it beats powerfully up and down. Although it is not the ocean's fastest swimmer, a dugong can reach speeds of 5 to 6 miles (8 to 10 km) per hour. But at higher speeds, it soon gets tired.

When a dugong wants to slow down or stop, it holds out its front flippers as a brake. To turn one way or the other, it twists its tail flukes and steers itself with its flippers. When it swims faster, the dugong holds its flippers tightly beside its body, making its shape even more streamlined. But most of the time, a dugong is content to swim along just under the surface of the water at a gentle, leisurely pace, with its flippers hanging down below its body.

A dugong uses its
flippers to steer.

Mates

When female dugongs are about 9 to 10 years old, they are mature enough to bear young. Often, as many as 20 male dugongs, or **bulls**, compete with one another for a **mate**. They show off to gain the attention of a lone female. During this time, the males become very **boisterous**, rolling over and lunging in the water and making loud splashing noises with their tail. All the while, the female tries to shake off her pursuers, twisting and turning sharply to make an escape. Eventually, when one of the male dugongs has won this "contest," he mates with the female. Female dugongs are pregnant for up to 13 to 14 months before they give birth.

A New Dugong

The dugong mother gives birth to her young in shallow water, just beneath the surface. She only has one baby, or **calf**, at a time. Like other sea mammals that are born in the water, dugong calves are normally born tail-first. If they were born headfirst, their natural instinct to breathe immediately might cause them to drown. When they are born tail-first, the calf can swim straight to the surface to take a breath.

Baby dugongs arrive in the world as perfect little replicas of their parents, fully alert with their eyes open. The mother may help her calf by gently pushing it in the right direction. In the first few hours of the calf's life, the mother "teaches" it the swimming, submerging, and breathing cycle necessary for its survival.

A dugong needs to eat up to 15 percent of its body weight in food each day.

A dugong calf stays close to its mother for protection in the first few years of its life.

Feeding Baby

At birth, dugong calves measure about 3 feet (1 m) long and weigh between 44 and 77 pounds (20 to 35 kg)—that's about ten times the weight of a newborn human baby. Their skin is pale brown in color when they are born. The skin gradually turns darker as the calves mature. Adult dugong skin color is dark gray. After it takes a breath of air, the dugong calf drinks milk from its mother for the first time. Although the calf is able to eat sea grasses very soon after it is born, it continues to nurse from its mother for some time. The calf often drinks its mother's milk while she continues to swim and graze.

Bonding

Dugong mothers and calves form a close bond. They often swim together within touching distance, only a few inches apart. Sometimes, the dugong calf positions itself just above its mother as they swim together. Swimming in its mother's "slipstream" might help the young calf make progress in the water. Staying close to its mother, the calf does not need to beat its tail as much, so it uses up less energy. Sometimes, the mother swims near the surface of the water, making it easy for her young calf to take gulps of air. A mother and her offspring may stay close together for several years, perhaps until the next calf is born in three to seven years' time.

By swimming above its mother, the dugong calf can swim more quickly in the water.

A family group of dugongs
feeds together on the
seabed off the coast of
Western Australia.

38

Family

Dugongs are often seen swimming alone. But scientists think that, like other marine mammals and humans, dugongs may be sociable animals. That means dugongs probably spend some of their time feeding and swimming together as a family group. A dugong family may consist of an adult male, an adult female, and one or two dugong calves. Sometimes dugongs swim together in a very large group called a **herd**. They may get together in such large numbers in areas where there is plentiful sea grass and other tasty plants for them to feast on. Dugongs have been seen swimming in a kind of formation, in the same way that orcas and dolphins swim together.

Threatened Dugongs

Dugongs are shy, timid creatures. They're not aggressive to other animals and have no real way to defend themselves from attack. They tend to stay mainly in shallow waters and avoid **predators**, such as sharks and orcas, that live in the deeper parts of the ocean. The greatest threat to dugongs is not from other animals but from humans. In some parts of the world, dugongs are hunted and killed for their meat and their **blubber**, which contains oils. Dugong skin has also been used for leather, and their tusks are sometimes carved into ornaments and other objects. In some areas, dugongs are now protected. Unfortunately, efforts to protect them are not always successful.

This dugong was probably once attacked by a shark, since part of its tail is missing.

Dugongs are well insulated from the cold with a thick layer of fat on their body.

Insulation

Some animals have thick fur or hair to keep out the cold. Birds have feathers for the same reason. To stay warm in the water, dugongs and other marine mammals, such as whales, have special insulation on their body. Under their smooth, outer skin is a very thick layer of fat, called blubber. Blubber prevents heat from being lost and stops dugongs from feeling the cold. Because dugongs live in warm, tropical oceans, they need less blubber than whales. Even so, much of a dugong's body weight consists of this insulating blubber.

Communication

Because dugongs' eyesight is not especially good, they don't rely too much on their sense of vision to help find their way around in the murky waters. But dugongs do have very good hearing. They may be able to hear sounds made by other dugongs. Because sound waves travel farther underwater than in the air, communicating with noises is the best way for dugongs to locate one another. Dugong sounds have been described as "bleats" or "whistles," similar to those of dolphins. Some of the sounds made by dugongs are at such a low pitch that humans are unable to hear them. Scientists have made recordings of dugong noises.

Scientists think that dugongs probably use their sense of hearing to find their way around the ocean.

The sea grass around this manatee's head can be mistaken for long hair.

Mermaids?

There is a story that tells of sailors on long voyages who confused dugongs with mermaids. A mermaid is a mythical creature with the head and upper body of a beautiful woman and the tail of a fish. So why did sailors mistake dugongs for mermaids? One explanation is that sailors saw dugong mothers caring for their young, not unlike human mothers. Another possible explanation is that sailors mistook the seaweed attached to a dugong's head for a mermaid's flowing hair!

Protecting Dugongs

In many areas, dugongs are now an endangered species. This means that they could soon become extinct unless humans work to help them survive. Scientists believe that in many places the numbers of dugongs are declining. The growth of towns and cities along the coasts often leads to pollution. Pollution damages the sea-grass beds that are the dugongs' main source of food. Along with the destruction of their **habitat**, dugongs risk being caught accidentally in fishing nets. Trapped in the nets, dugongs are unable to get to the surface for air and they drown. **Conservation** is helping dugongs survive, and hopefully flourish, in Great Barrier Reef Marine Park in Australia. There, thousands of these gentle creatures live peacefully in protected conditions.

Words to Know

Adapted	Changed to better suit a habitat.
Aquatic	Living in water.
Bacteria	Tiny microscopic organisms. Some kinds of bacteria cause diseases.
Blubber	A layer of fat beneath a sea mammal's skin that keeps it warm in water.
Boisterous	Noisy and playful.
Bulls	Male dugongs.
Calf	A young dugong.
Conservation	Preserving habitats and the animals and plants that live there.
Digest	To break down food in the body.
Equator	An imaginary circle around the earth, midway between the North and South Poles.
Evolution	Process of gradual change over a long time.
Extinction	When all of a kind of animal has died out and is gone forever.
Flippers	The front paddlelike limbs of a dugong.

49

Flukes	Tail fins.
Gills	Structures in the head of fish that allow them to breathe underwater.
Graze	To eat grass.
Habitat	The type of place where an animal or plant lives.
Herbivores	Animals that eat mainly plants.
Herd	A group of dugongs.
Mammals	Animals with fur or hair on their body that feed their young milk.
Marine	Relating to the sea.
Mate	Either of a breeding pair of animals.
Molars	Teeth used for crushing and grinding.
Offspring	The young of an animal.
Predators	Animals that hunt other animals.
Species	The scientific word for animals of the same kind that breed together.
Streamlined	Smooth and sleek, able to move through water or air easily.

Find Out More

Books

Martin, P. A. F. *Manatees*. True Books: Animals. Danbury, Connecticut: Children's Press, 2003.

Ripple, J. *Manatees and Dugongs of the World*. Stillwater, Minnesota: Voyageur Press, 2002.

Web sites

Dugong
animals.nationalgeographic.com/animals/mammals/dugong.html
A profile of the dugong.

Dugongs
www.enchantedlearning.com/subjects/mammals/manatee/Dugongprintout.shtml
Information about dugongs and a picture to print.

Index